The planets

CONTENTS

About the planets..................................2

Mercury..4

Venus...6

Earth..8

Mars...10

Jupiter..12

Saturn..14

Uranus...16

Neptune...18

Pluto..20

About the planets

Nine planets travel around the Sun. Four of the planets are huge. Four are small. The ninth planet, Pluto, is the smallest planet of all.

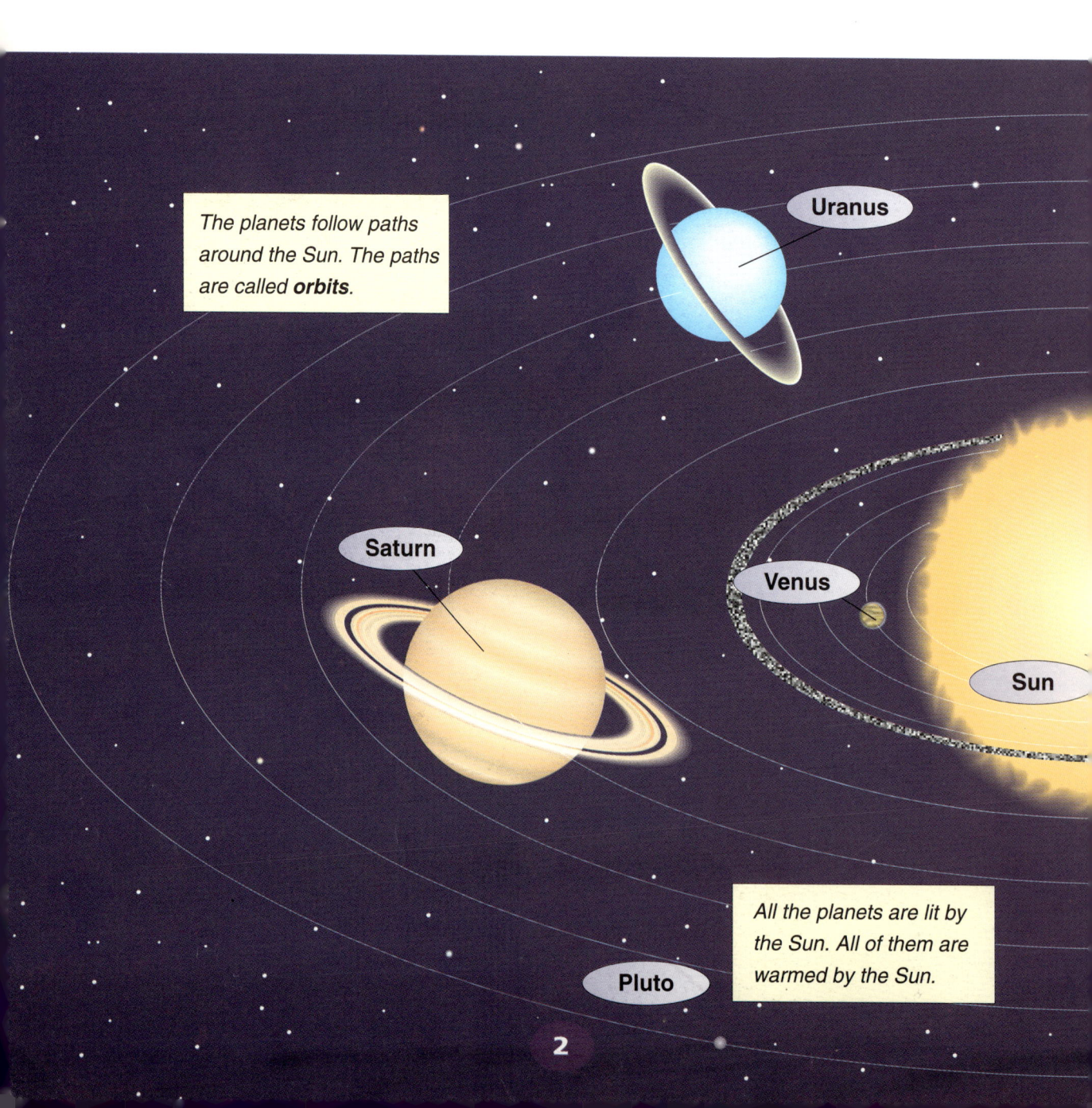

The planets follow paths around the Sun. The paths are called **orbits**.

Uranus

Saturn

Venus

Sun

Pluto

All the planets are lit by the Sun. All of them are warmed by the Sun.

Most of the planets have moons travelling around them. Some planets have bits of ice, rock and dust going around them as well.

Earth

Jupiter

Mars

Mercury

Neptune

All the planets go around the Sun in the same direction.

Mercury

Mercury is a small, pinky-brown, rocky planet. It spins very slowly. In the day Mercury is extremely hot. At night it is extremely cold.

Mercury's surface is covered in large holes called **craters**. Most of the craters were made by rocks falling from space a long time ago. The rocks crashed on to Mercury and exploded. The explosions made the craters.

Planet facts: Mercury

Made of
rock with a centre of iron

Size
4878 kilometres across (about three times smaller than Earth)

Moons
none

Average distance from the Sun
58 million kilometres

Craters on the surface of Mercury

5

Venus

Venus is the nearest planet to Earth. In some ways it is Earth's twin. It is about the same size. It is made of rock. It has winds and clouds.

In other ways, Venus is very different from Earth. The clouds are thick and yellow. They completely cover Venus. They are made of tiny drops of acid. Underneath the clouds Venus is scorching hot. It has strangely shaped volcanoes and deep canyons. It is covered in orange rocks and dust.

The first robot spacecraft to land on Venus lasted one hour. Then the heat melted it.

Planet facts: Venus

Made of
rock with a centre of iron

Size
12 102 kilometres across (about the same size as Earth)

Moons
none

Average distance from the Sun
108 million kilometres

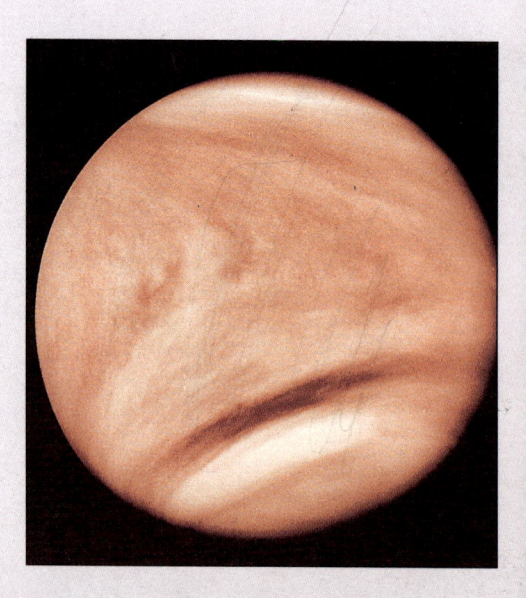

This picture has been made using a computer. The surface of Venus probably looks like this.

Earth

Water covers most of Earth's surface. Thick ice covers the Arctic and the Antarctic. Earth has earthquakes and erupting volcanoes. Its rocks are worn away by wind and rain. All the time, new rocks are being made.

Each planet is different. Each planet has things the other planets don't have. Earth has living plants and creatures. So far, living things have not been found on any other planet.

Earth has one moon. The Moon is only a bit smaller than Mercury. It is rocky and covered in dust. It has no air, no water, and no life.

Planet facts: Earth

Made of
rock with a centre of iron

Size
12 756 kilometres across (the largest rocky planet)

Moons
one

Average distance from the Sun
150 million kilometres

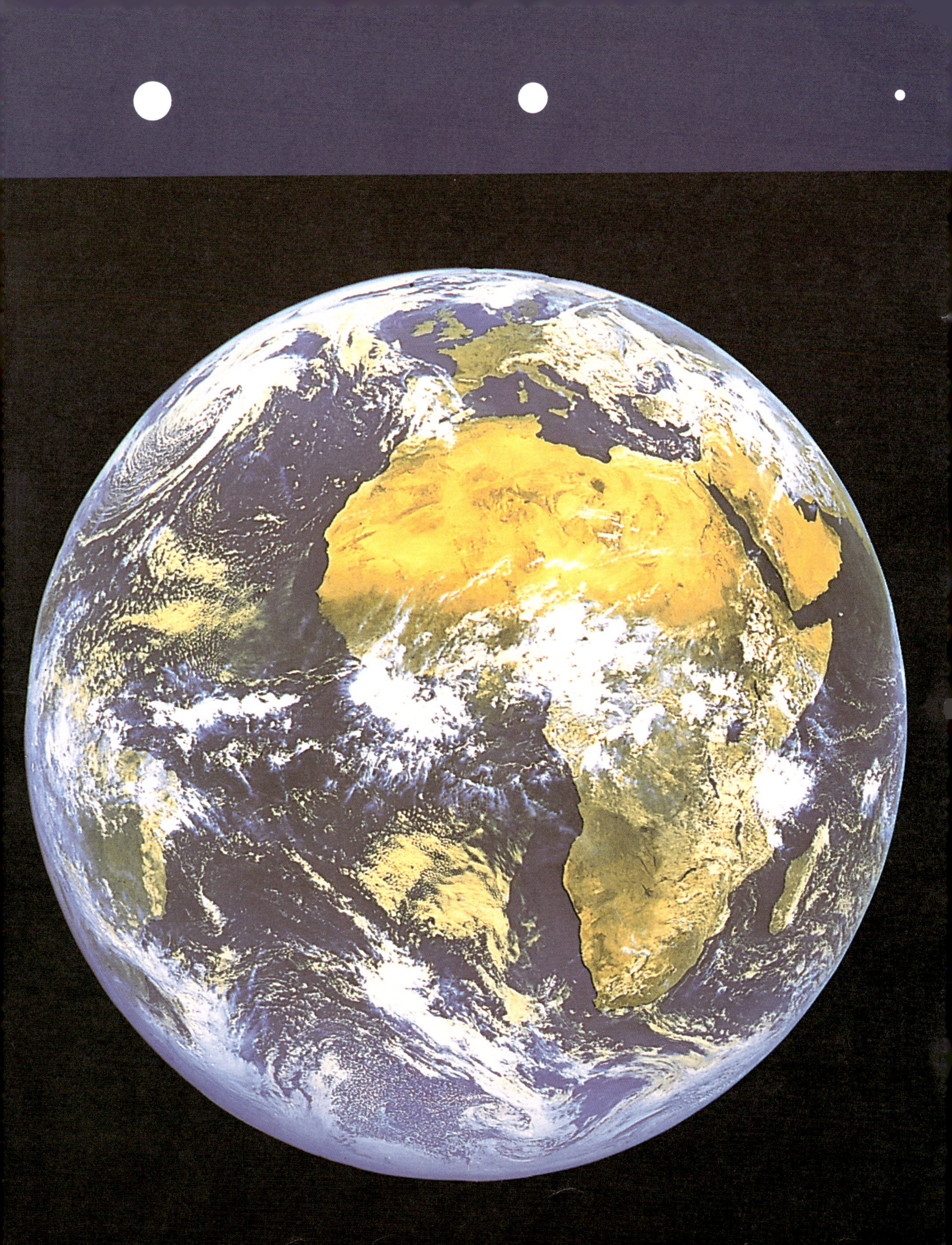

Mars

Once Mars was warm and wet. Now it is cold and dry. Once there were rivers. Now there are only dry river beds. Mars has red, sandy soil. Winds blow the soil up into the air. The soil makes the sky look pink.

Mars has many big, old volcanoes. A huge canyon splits the surface of Mars.

Mars has two tiny rocky moons. In 100 million years, one of them will crash into Mars. It will make a giant crater.

Planet facts: Mars

Made of
rock with a centre of iron

Size
6786 kilometres across
(half as wide as Earth)

Moons
two

Average distance from the Sun
228 million kilometres

A photograph of the surface of Mars

11

Jupiter

Jupiter is an enormous ball of gases. All the other planets could fit inside with room to spare. It spins around faster than any other planet. Orange and white clouds swirl around Jupiter. There are storms and flashes of lightning. Jupiter has a ring around it made of tiny pieces of dust.

Jupiter has 16 moons. Four of them are as big as planets. One is smooth and white. It is covered in ice. Another is red, orange and yellow.

Planet facts: Jupiter

Made of
melted rock centre, surrounded by liquid and gas

Size
143 000 kilometres across
(11 times wider than Earth)

Moons
16

Average distance from the Sun
778 million kilometres

Jupiter with two of its moons

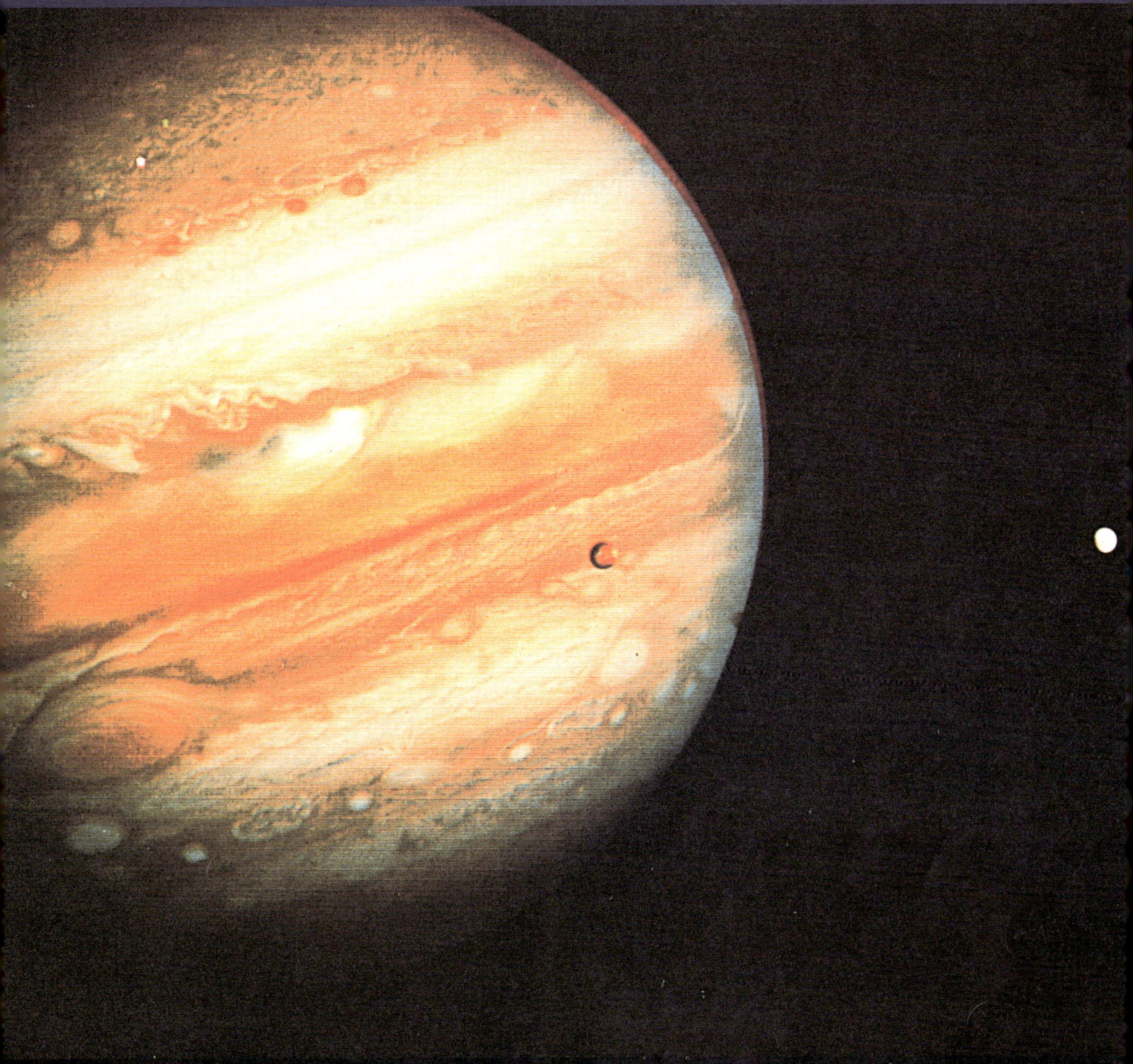

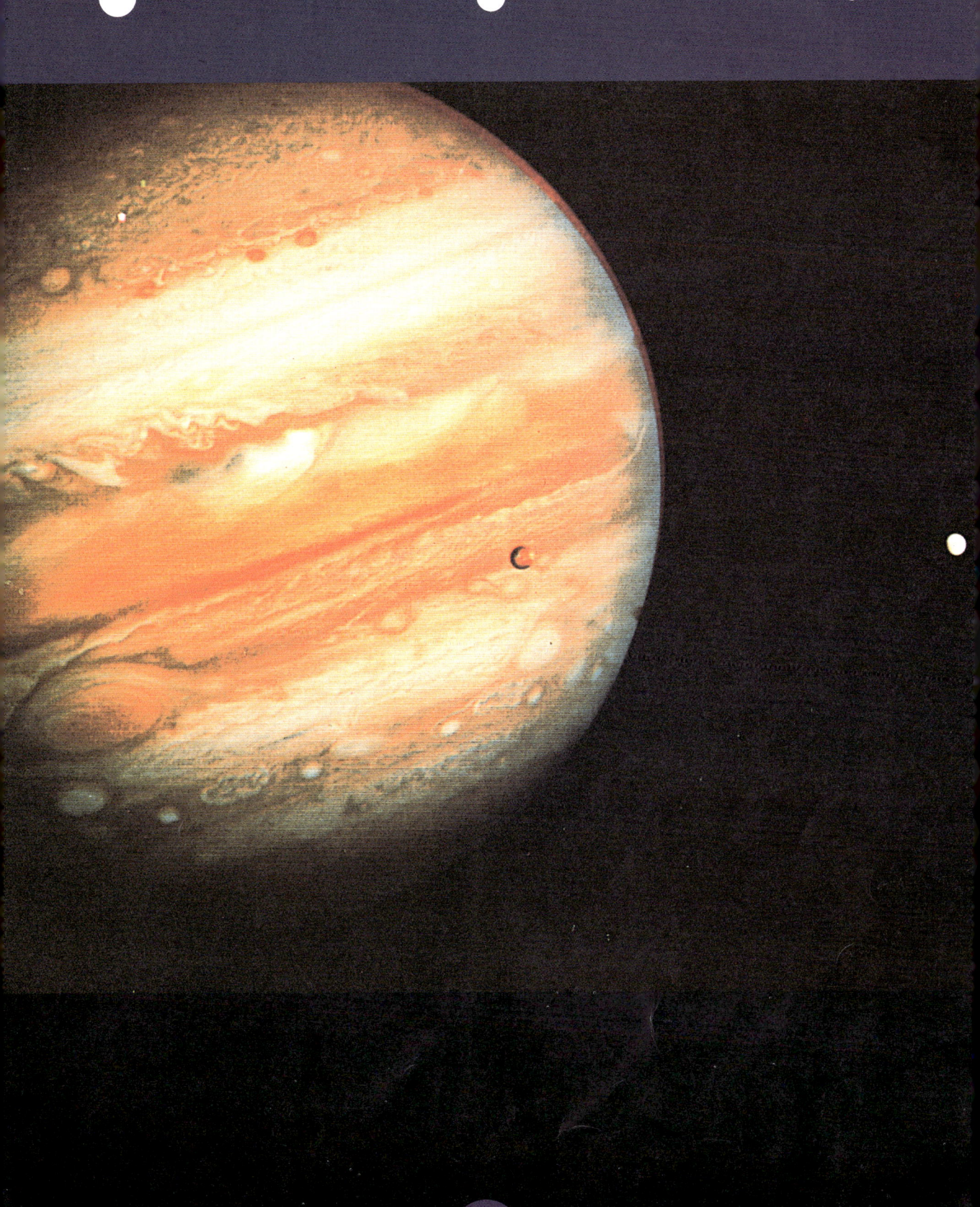

Saturn

Saturn is a gas giant like Jupiter. It is not as large as Jupiter. Only 850 Earths could fit inside Saturn. Jupiter could hold 1400 Earths.

At least 17 moons travel around Saturn. Some of the moons have huge craters. Scientists think that once there was another moon. A giant **meteorite** smashed it into bits. Some of the bits were as big as buses. Some were only specks.

The bits made rings around Saturn. The rings can be seen from Earth through a telescope. They look rather like ears or handles.

Planet facts: Saturn

Made of
rocky centre surrounded by liquid and gas

Size
120 536 kilometres across
(10 times wider than Earth)

Moons
17

Average distance from the Sun
1427 million kilometres

15

Uranus

Uranus is a huge ball of dirty water. It spins around fast, tipped on its side. Under the water is ice. Its centre is hot rock. From space Uranus looks like a smooth blue-green ball. Nothing shows on it, not even a cloud.

Uranus has thin narrow rings. The rings are made of black rocky lumps. It has 15 small moons. They are made of rock and ice. On some of the moons there are high mountains, giant cliffs, large cracks and strange markings. No-one knows why the moons are like this. No-one knows why Uranus spins on its side.

Planet facts: Uranus

Made of
rock surrounded by ice and water

Size
51 120 kilometres across (about four times wider than Earth)

Moons
15

Average distance from the Sun
2 870 million kilometres

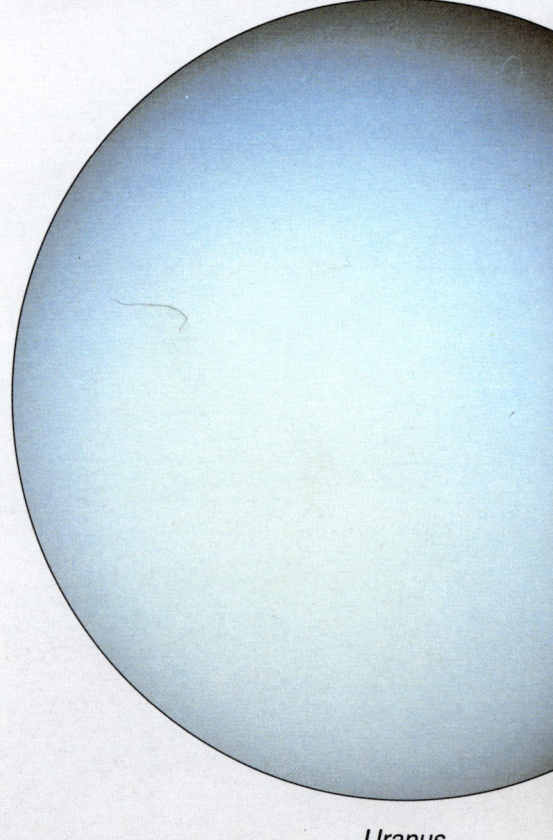

Uranus

The surface of Miranda, one of Uranus's moons

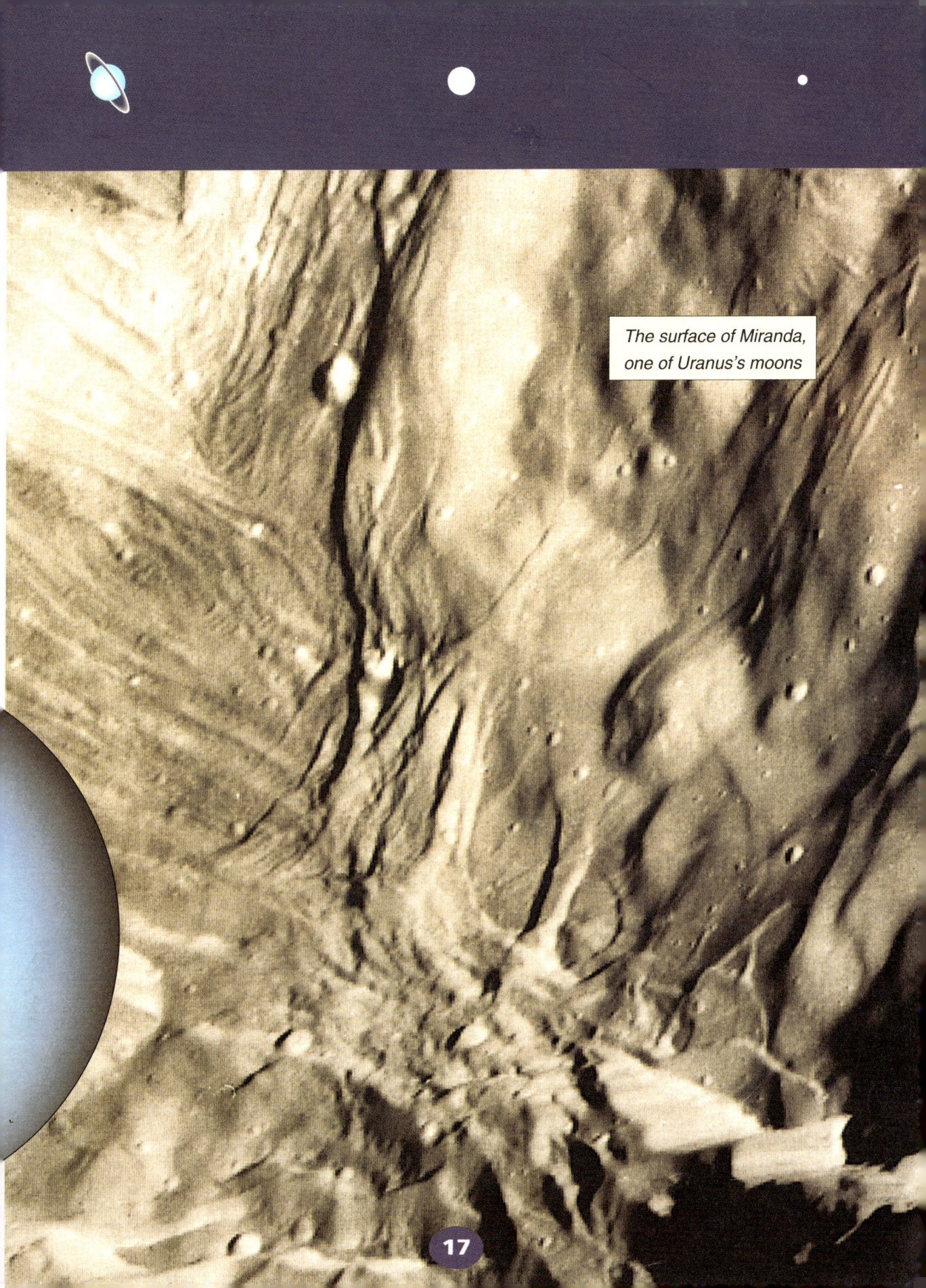

Neptune

Neptune is a big ball of water, like Uranus. It also has a hot rocky centre. But Neptune is very different from Uranus. Giant storms sweep around it. The winds are extremely fast.

Neptune has a few rings made of black rocks and dust.

Neptune has a very strange moon called Triton. Triton is made of ice and rock. Black smoke shoots out from the ice.

Planet facts: Neptune

Made of
hot rock at the centre, surrounded by water

Size
49 528 kilometres across (about four times wider than Earth)

Moons
eight

Average distance from the Sun
4497 million kilometres

The surface of Triton

19

Pluto

Pluto is a very small planet. It is a reddish colour and has one large grey moon. Pluto and its moon are very close to each other.

Spacecraft from Earth have not visited Pluto yet. They have visited every other planet.

There might be other planets beyond Pluto. They have not been discovered yet.

Even the most powerful telescopes on Earth only show Pluto and its moon as little blobs.

Planet facts: Pluto

Made of
rock and frozen water

Size
2280 kilometres across (smaller than Earth's Moon)

Moons
one (half as wide as Pluto)

Average distance from the Sun
5914 million kilometres